To: Selena Ow[e]
In the WORD (J[ ]
the devil the Flesh and the
world.
Love,
Evangelist Vera Armstrong
6-16-2016

EXHORTATIONS
TO PRAY

Vera Armstrong

770 -
R.t.J

313 - 467 - 9550
Chy.

931-533-9711
Ben

678 964-9814
Daisha

Exhortations to Pray

Copyright © 2015 by Vera Armstrong

Printed in the United States of America

Book cover designed by:
EverlastingDeZigns.com

Reference: The Holy Bible

Editorial work done by: LaToya Williams
@PiecesOfMeEditorial 419-322-0438

Author's Information:
Phone: 419-309-2805
Email: holyngod@yahoo.com

Table of Contents

Forward   4

Acknowledgements   6

Dedication   10

Preface   12

Introduction   14

The Importance of Love and Faith   22

Why is it Important to be Clean   44

Thanksgiving and Praise   52

Obedience in Prayer   62

Why must we pray?   69

When should we pray?   75

Our Position in Prayer   83

Free to Establish   95

Prayers of Distinction   102

Exercise   121

About The Author   127

Forward

I generally don't have time to read all the books that so many people send me, but I am very happy and honored to be able to endorse my dear friend Vera Armstrong's book. I have known Vera for many years she has been a great service to me and the Congregation that I Shepherd. She is someone that not only teaches about prayer but she is also a woman who prays. In her Book Exhortations to Pray; Vera covers the foundations of having a vibrant prayer life through and in the LORD. She speaks about the importance of Love in prayer and how important it is to have Faith when we are praying. The posture of our hearts when we pray; how un-forgiveness can block us from moving God's Heart. How important it is to make a willful decision to pray with Thanksgiving as the Scriptures says. She speaks about prayer as an opportunity to praise the One that gave us the lips to praise Him. I heartily endorse my friend Vera Armstrong's Book and also endorse the testimony of her life. She is the one that is qualified to write a book on prayer. I encourage you to read Exhortations to Pray.

Rabbi Kirt A. Schneider

Acknowledgements

There's a vast array of people whom God has raised up to be a blessing and make deposits in me. They have encouraged me to go forth to do my Father's will for my life. Some of the people I know personally and some of the people have never even heard of me. But I want them to share in this great moment in my life.

To my wonderful husband James:
God has given you the ability to deal with me. I thank you for his love and patience and especially for challenging me every day. You have caused me to seek God on a continuous basis (smile). May God bless and keep you always. (James is now deceased.)

To my wonderful son, James Jr.:
You were a blessing to raise. You obeyed

most of the rules. Just want you to know I'm proud of you. May you be highly favored of the Lord.

To my mother Jennie:
You raised me to have character, and integrity, Thank you. To all my family members who contributed to my life in one way or another, may God bless you each exceedingly and abundantly above all you may ask or think...(Ephesians 3:20). (My Mother is now deceased.)

To the spiritual leaders in my life:
My wonderful Bishop, Andrew Merritt, and his humble wife, Pastor Viveca Merritt, I thank God for their obedience to Him. No matter what storm comes upon them they persevere with tenacity in always believing and trusting God to do that which he said He would. They have been an inspiration to

me. I thank God for them. I pray that He bless them, always.

To my colleagues in The United
Prayer Ministry

God placed me with for a season, I thank God for each one's ability to know what their purpose is and we can all come together to fulfill the complete purpose of God for our lives. God bless you all.

To those spiritual gifts in God's
kingdom whom I have had the opportunity to
share in their ministry:

God has given them in one way or another. Some of them know nothing about me but I just want to say thank you for paying the price for the anointing upon your lives. Pastor Fred Price, Evangelist Jackie McCullough, Pastor Kenneth and Gloria Copeland, Missionary JoAnna Rochester, Pastor John Cherry, Pastor Wayne Powell,

Bishop Thomas Jakes, Dr. Myles Munroe, and Minister Donnie McClurkin. Thank you and may the blessings of the Lord always be upon you.

Dedication

I would like to dedicate this book of inspiring and encouraging **"Exhortations to Pray"** first and foremost to my Father, Almighty God who created me, my Lord and Savior Jesus Christ who died for me, and my helper the Holy Spirit who leads and guides me into all truths. Thank you with much gratitude and love. **"Exhortations to Pray"** is also dedicated to all of you intercessors around the world who daily stands in the gap for the needs of the people. I give God all the praise for those of you that heard His call and responded in obedience to Him.

In *Isaiah 59:16 "And He saw that there was no man, and wondered that there was no Intercessor: Therefore His arm brought salvation unto Him; and His righteousness, it sustained Him."* Since God did not see a man that was interceding on behalf of others, He had to send a man, Hallelujah! And that man was Jesus (thank you Father). Jesus took upon Himself our transgressions, all our iniquities and sins, and in so doing He brought us Salvation and Righteousness. Jesus is our example for His work of redemption is complete, and He is now seated at the Right Hand of God interceding on our behalf. Jesus said "that we would do greater works than He." Since He suffered for us to obtain our rightful place, and has now given us this charge to do greater works than He, then the least we can do is pray as He prayed and is still praying.

I thank God that this book will help those of us who have not prayed as we ought. It will help us to make a complete turn-around in our prayer life to the glory of God. (Amen).

Preface

"If my people, which are called by my name, shall humble themselves, and pray, and seek my face, and turn from their wicked ways; then will I hear from heaven, and will forgive their sin and will heal their land. Now mine eyes shall be open, and mine ears attentive unto the prayer that is made in this place."

II Chronicles 7:14-15

If the least of the saints would do this, the devil and his forces would be in serious trouble. As joint heirs, with Jesus, according to (Matthew 18:18) we have the ability to bind and loose. The keys to The Kingdom of God are at our disposal. (Hallelujah!!!).

It's very simplistic what God wants us to do. In *Zechariah 4:6 "Then He answered and spake unto me (saying, this is the word of the LORD unto Zerubbabel, saying, Not by might, nor by power, but by my spirit, saith the LORD of hosts.)*

For it is not on our ability that we do anything; it's total reliance on the Father, Son, and the Holy Spirit. When we alleviate ourselves of the flesh and operate totally in the Spirit, we'll see God do what He has promised us. Therefore, the devil has no authority over us. If we take heed to do as Jesus did the Body of Christ will be one.

Introduction

On October 25, 1994, early on a very cold morning (inside and out), there was no power on in our home, because our electricity was off. While I was asleep with many garments on to keep warm, and the bed was heavy with covers, the Holy Spirit awakened me and whispered in my soul, "Now is the time to release your potential." As I lay there thinking what I could do to release this potential and to get out of this syndrome of lack in our lives, God gave me ideas that would portray His abundance. He showed me how there was something He had already given me, and that all I had to do was release them in book form.

This idea had come to me before, but I just shrugged it off, thinking God is not telling me to do this. But now I know God has told me to do this, for not only will others be blessed and encouraged, but it will also bless me and my family. Praises be to God!

Through trials and adverse circumstances, if we remain in tune to our Father, he will show us what to do in the midst of them all, I said, "All!!!!"

God told me several years ago that I would prosper by the diligence of my own hands. Working a secular job is not just what God had for me, but there was something else that God specifically had for me to do in order to help others and to glorify Him; He had a spiritual work also.

It has been almost three weeks since we have been without electricity. There has been no TV playing, no cooking, no unnecessary burning of electrical lights, and no hot curling of hair every day, and those are just a few things one cannot do when there is no electricity. Oh, but God continues to speak to our hearts no matter what we are going through; for nothing can separate us from His love. I have learned that trials come (I know there are scriptures in the Bible that teach us about trials and tribulation, but until you have lived through and had victory over trials, it will just be scripture to you) to help us no matter how we feel about them, no matter what people say about us, and no matter how the devil attacks us. We must continue to pray and trust God; for He knows exactly what He is doing.

I must say this has been one of the hardest times we have ever been through (each one gets harder). You cry, you pray and continue to believe God. You cry, you pray, and continue to trust God. You cry, you pray, and continue to wait on God. You cry, you pray, and continue to thank God.

You cry, you pray, and continue to worship God. You cry, you pray, and continue to praise God. You cry, you pray, and continue to have faith in God to do what He says He'll do. This keeps you <u>sane</u>. This helps you to <u>endure</u> the shame and the pain. Let's face it! If you are known as a prayer warrior and are attacked in your personal stuff, it is humiliating. Not so much because of what people (saints) say, but because the devil uses it to try and make you feel inadequate in what God has given you to do. But the devil is a liar!!! And Jesus is Lord!

To make a long story short, if we had not gone through this time of suffering, and endured, this book would not have been released. Suffering helps us to get out of ourselves and hear a clear word from the Lord. (Amen.)

I thank God for the way He has allowed different circumstances to come in order that what He wants out of us we'll be able to release it so it can help others. God is the one who gives talents, abilities, and gifts to be used for His glory and His glory only.

May the love of God be shed abroad in each of your hearts, as it is in mine. Let it be to the point where we'll lay down our lives for the brethren. For remember, He who loves the most, prays the best. Praise God!

What is prayer?

Prayer is the act or practice of praying to God. I am talking about the I Am that I Am God, the Creator of the Heaven and the Earth. He is the Almighty God, The One who is and was and is to come. He is the one who made us in His image and likeness. It is an earnest request, an entreaty, supplication a humble and sincere request to

God. Prayer is an utterance to Him in praise, thanksgiving, and confession (etc.). It is any spiritual communication with God. It's a dialogue where we talk to Him and He talks back to us giving us instructions for our lives.

Religion is *universal* and *ineradicable* so is prayer, for people everywhere seek a relationship when realizing their dependence on a higher order no matter what their understanding of it is. Whether it's primitive or sophisticated, gross spiritual or anthropomorphic, it's how humans identify with God.

The Bible supplies abundant evidence of the fact that people cry out.

Examples:

I Kings 18:26-29 (Idol worshippers)

Acts 17:15-23 (The learned idolaters of Athens prayed)

Psalm 65:1-5 (David cried out for help and mercy).

Luke 3:21-22, 5:16, 9:18; John 17 (Jesus prayed).

2 Corinthians 5:17; Galatians 5:20; Psalm 139:1-2, 13-16; Philippians 3:3- 11(Prayer gives us Identity)

Philippians 4:13; Ecclesiastes 12:13; 1 Peter 2:4-5; Daniel 7:18 (Prayer gives us Purpose)

Matthew 5:1-12; Mark 16:15-20; Jeremiah 29:11-14 (Prayer gives us Focus)

Matthew 6:6 (None of us can be useful to
God in the public sphere, if we are not
putting Him first in our private lives.)

*Nothing is going to be accomplished
for God in this hour unless it is first
accomplished in prayer*

~Vera Armstrong~

The Importance of Love and Faith When We Pray

What is Love?

"If I have the gift of being able to speak in other languages without learning them and could speak in every language there is in heaven and earth but didn't love others, I would only be making noise. If I had the gift of prophecy and knew all about what is going to happen in the future, knew everything about everything, but didn't love others, what good would it do? Even if I had the gift of faith so that I could speak to a mountain and make it move, I would still be worth nothing at all without love. If I gave everything I have to poor people, and if I were burned alive for preaching the Gospel but didn't love others, it would be of no value whatever. Love is very patient and kind, never jealous or envious, never boastful or proud, never haughty or selfish

or rude. Love does not demand its own way. It is not irritable or touchy. Does not hold grudges and will hardly even notice when others do it wrong. It is never glad about injustice, but rejoices whenever truth wins out. If you love someone you will be loyal to him no matter what the cost. You will always believe in him, always expect the best of him, and always stand your ground in defending him. All the special gifts and powers from God will someday come to an end, but Love goes on forever."

(I Corinthians 13:1-8 (TLB))

When we pray for others, love should always be the motive; imagine that someone wronged you (Christian or Heathen) terribly. Let's say, for instance if your character was attacked, that's very personal. to start your prayer time, that person comes across your mind but you dismiss them quickly from your thoughts.

You're saying to yourself I'm not going to pray for them because of what they did to me. Well, in James 5:20 God says *"Let him know, that he which covereth the sinner from the error of his way shall save a soul from death, and shall hide a multitude of sins."* I Peter 4:8 *says, "And above all things have fervent charity among yourselves: for charity shall cover the multitude of sins."*

Believe me; that which was done to you if it did not bless you, then rest assured it was sinning whether it was a Christian or a heathen that did it. So our main concern here is not what was done to us but covering that person's soul, by praying for them because we can love our neighbors as ourselves. Don't you want to be forgiven by others for what you did to them?

It is so essential to operate in love when we pray, because not only do we cover another person's soul, we are being obedient to what God has told us to do.

If we love other Christians it proves that we have been delivered from hell and given eternal life. But a person who doesn't have love for others is headed for eternal death (I John 3:14, TLB).

Love is not just something you say to people or project as you pray for them. Love is doing what needs to be done. Have you ever known anyone who had a specific need, whether it was physical, spiritual, emotional, or financial? You were the only one that knew about it, but you did nothing when there was something you could have done. Let's suppose that person was a baby Christian and you were the only one they knew years before as the "Christian". Now they've come into the knowledge that according to God's word that Christians love and help one another. They share their problem with you, which by the way happens to be financial, but remember, they are a baby Christian and have not totally learned to trust God. Now you send them away without even trying to help. What do you suppose they are thinking at this point? But if someone who is supposed to be a Christian has enough money to live well, and sees a brother in need and won't help him, how can God's love be within him?

"Little children, let us stop just saying we love people; let us really love them, and show it by our actions. Then we will know for sure, by our actions that we are on God's side. And our conscious will be clear even when we stand before the Lord".

I John 3:17-19 (TLB).

When I talk about loving others I'm not just talking about loving your immediate family members or your brothers and sisters in Christ, the others also include the heathen. I say this because God has taught me this from experience:

Testimony:

A while ago I worked for this company and the other workers were not nice to me. They gave me memos after the fact, and I was not trained properly for my position. They did not respect my property, and these are just a few things that were done to me. In the midst of all this unrighteousness, I never verbalized my feelings to them. This irresponsible treatment from them continued for several months. Then one day, I could no longer take it anymore. I went to the manager of the company and told what had been happening to me all those months. The manager was shocked, appalled, and also angry. For this type of treatment towards another employee was against company policy and warranted dismissal.

To alleviate me from any more hardships, they moved me to another place to work. Well I thought, "This is great!" The people at this other place were wonderful. They taught me everything in a few days that I should have had months before but was never given access to. Needless to say, I was very happy. After being there for a while and management saw how well I progressed, they decided to send me back to my original company. Hearing this news made me very angry. So after my last day there, while driving home alone, I started yelling how I wasn't going back to the other place to work because those people were so mean and unfair to me. They were just a bunch of heathens anyway! I didn't need to be around them anymore. After carrying on like that for a while, the Holy Spirit quietly spoke six words to me. They were: "Jesus died for the whole world." He did not say another word then. He let me know that if I had been the only one in the world Jesus still would have died for me."

The next day the Holy Spirit reassured me that Jesus did not just die for Christians who have already accepted Him, but He died for every person that had been on this Earth, who was already on this Earth, and those that were going to come to this Earth. Naturally, that changed my mind, and God sent me back there to let those people see the love of Jesus in me. I had to intercede for them daily in order that they may not be lost. For now the seed had been planted and in due season that seed will spring forth.

That's why now I'm so careful never to forget from whence I came.

"There was a time when some of you were just like that but now your sins are washed away, and you are set apart for God, and He has accepted you because of what the Lord Jesus Christ and The Spirit of our God have done for you".

(I Corinthians 6:11, L.B.)

As Christians God expects us to obey the principals He has given us. We who have already been born again have the responsibility to see that others know about Christ and that He died for them also. In John 13:34-35 (KJV), Jesus is speaking and He said, *"A new commandment I give to you, that ye love one another. By this all will know that ye are my disciples, if ye have love, one to another."*

After all, we did not bring any money with us when we came into this world, and we can't carry away a single penny when we die. For the love of money is the first step toward all kinds of sin. Do not let your affections of love be in the wrong place.

God does not want us to be selfish towards one another. We are to be kind and share with one another.

"Now the company of believers was of one heart and soul, and not one of them claimed that anything which he possessed was [exclusively] his own, but everything they had was in common and for the use of all. And with great strength and ability and power the Apostles delivered their testimony to the resurrection of the Lord Jesus Christ, and great grace (loving-kindness and favor and goodwill) rested richly upon them all. Nor was there a destitute or needy person among them, for as many as were owners of

lands or houses proceeded to sell them, and one by one they brought (gave back) the amount received from the sales, And laid it at the feet of the Apostles (special messengers). Then distribution was made according as anyone had need".

Acts 4:32-35, Amplified Bible

When you walk in love selfishness has no part in your life. You will have no problem in sharing anything that you have.

My mother raised us with good, sound Christian principals. The main one is to have concern for one another. We were taught that all people are somebody and no one person is better than another no matter what they do, how much money they have, or what their Pedigree is. We all have the same basic need and that is to be loved. We all need Jesus too, whether we want Him or not. Jesus established the Church in order that we may continue to build on its foundation which is love!!

In order to be able to bless others we must first bless the Lord. Blessings stem from love, how can one bless if he does not love?

"He, who does not love, does not know God, for God is love. Beloved if God so loved us, we also ought to love one another".

I John 4:8-11, KJV

How can we know God in order to know how to love Him? Well, give your life to Him as a sacrifice. Be faithful in love, fasting, praying, and also put away the accursed things.

Once we have made a total commitment to God, then we will know the pure love of God. That love then spills out all over, and there will be more than enough to go around. Therefore, no matter what happens in our lives, we will still be able to love others and God.

"For in whom are hidden all the treasures of wisdom and knowledge, as you have therefore received Christ Jesus the Lord, so walk in Him".

Colossians 2:3-4 KJV

Always be comfortable in the way God has made you, for we are all different and unique in our own way. Therefore, not knowing when you yourself may need the action of someone else's love, walk in the love of God, be yourself and always share. When we prioritize what sharing is all about, then we can keep it straight, thereby, not allowing selfishness to come into our lives in any way.

What are you doing for the Kingdom of God?

Is it Pastoring, Preaching, teaching, Missionary work, getting souls saved, Evangelizing, Prophesying, Organizing churches, praying for the sick, etc? My question to you is, are you doing it in love? Well, if we are doing all these wonderful things down here on Earth and up in Heaven God is shaking His head asking the question, why won't they love one another, as I have commanded? Don't they know that's why I sent my only begotten Son to die for them? It's because I love them." He had no sin but became sin for them. Why? Because of love! He took the penalty and the guilt of sin from them. Why? Because of love! Even now I say to them, *I John 1:9 LB, "If you confess your sins I'm faithful and just to forgive you of your sins and to cleanse you from all unrighteousness."* Why? Because of love!

On that day when all of us must stand before the Lord to give an account of what we did in our bodies and on this Earth, what do you really want Him to say to you?

Remember
No matter how many wonderful things we are doing for the Lord, if they are not done in love, the time and work you spent doing them was all in vain. I repeat in vain!

Prayer:

Father, forgive me for the times I have not shown love, walked in love, worked love, or even not loving towards others. Lord, I want to walk in your true love. Open my heart oh God that I might love as you love. I start this very moment to loving those whom I thought couldn't be loved. I thank you for continuing to love me even when I didn't love. Amen!

Faith

Now faith is the <u>substance</u> of things hoped for, the <u>evidence</u> of things not seen.

Hebrews 11:1 (KJV)

This is Webster's definition of substance: Substance is the real or essential part or element of anything; essence reality, or basic matter. It is the real content, meaning, or gist of something said or written, something that has independent existence, and is acted upon by causes or events; to be present. Look at this; by operating in faith generated by love we can bring that thing that's non-existence into something real. Then it will make itself present in the natural. Hallelujah!!!

Faith is Spirit, when we operate in faith we are walking in the Spirit. This is the realm where God is, that's why without faith we cannot please God.

Since, we are a three-part being Spirit, Soul, and Body. We hear God in our Spirit, The Spirit influences The Soul, for the Soul is the communicator between The Spirit and The Body. The Soul tells The Body what to do the Body (flesh) is the follower and does what The Soul tells it.

Prior to Salvation, The Soul Man was in charge. (Remember the song "I'm a Soul Man" well, we were). (Laugh)! The Spirit Man was dormant unable to function because it was disconnected from God because of the "Original Sin of Adam." The Soulish Realm consists of our will, intellect, emotions, senses, ego, pride, and all those things that can get us into a mess. Why do you suppose God wants and the devil also wants our Soul? The Soul is in charge of that which we know as our own power.

"This I say then, "walk in the Spirit, and ye shall not fulfill the lust of the flesh."

Galatians5:16-25 SFLB

The Word of God is Spirit. When we speak the Word, believe the Word, obey the Word, and act upon the Word, we will have our evidence. Evidence is the condition of being evident. It is to bear witness to; plainly visible or perceptible. Jesus said, "Only believe." When you pray and whatsoever you pray for believe that you have received, and then you shall have whatsoever you say.

You Say!!!!!!

Now, are you moving mountains with your faith?

There are many aspects of faith, great faith, mountain moving faith, little faith, etc.

"For all we need is faith working through love. Even with all your faith it must still be motivated by love. Faith works hand in hand with love you cannot have one without the other."

Galatians 5:6b (KJV)

If you have great faith to believe God for many possessions, like, status, freedom, Spiritual Authority, wealth, and health, and you do not love others, or help bless the ones who truly have a need. Then, your faith is in vain.

Think about God's Faith. Everything, He said, came into being. But what motivated God to say? His love is what motivates Him that's why faith had to <u>obey</u>. Let's face it we all have to come in the same way, through Jesus' love and kindness we are drawn. So draw someone by love and faith will. (Amen).

As we walk in love our faith takes a leap!

Testimony:

One morning while in my prayer closet, (after praying for others), I experienced a long period of silence in the presence of The LORD. Afterward I began to cry out to God for my own personal needs. It went from making petitions before God to asking how long this trial was going to last. Well, after what seemed like hours to me, God finally spoke.

He said, "Vera, this is what faith is". He showed me a vision of me standing on a very high ledge; it was so high I could not see the bottom. Then, He suspended a rope quite a distance from the ledge, which looked to me as though it was hanging from nothing. It looked that way to me because, I could see the top and the bottom part of the rope, it was just hanging there. Then He said, "This is what faith is", I want you to leap off this ledge and grab a hold of the rope. Now when you grab it hold on and don't let go.

Well, suffice to say my natural mind started to tell me if you do that then you are crazy. You will fall because that rope is not hanging onto anything. It was a brief battle with my mind and my Spirit, but, I came to the conclusion that the devil is a liar. You see the devil speaks to us in our mind, soulish realm. God speaks to our Spirit. Therefore, it's up to you and I which man is going to take action.

Well, after putting my mind into subjection to my Spirit I leaped off the ledge and grabbed the rope. Then God said, "now don't let go hold on no matter how hard the winds blow, or how many storms may come, hold on, even though you can't see me I'm here. For I am the Rope." Hallelujah!!

When the leap was made, an explosion occurred within my Inner Being that settled the issue in me. I know that God truly is "I Am" that "I Am". Praise Him!!

Prayer:

Father, I thank you that the entrance of Your Word brings light and understanding to the simple. I thank You Jesus that you are the Author and Finisher of my faith. I ask you Father to strengthen me to use my measure of faith for Your Glory. Forgive me for the times I did not exercise love to operate my faith. Also for not walking in faith to please You. Help me to always walk in love in order that I may have great faith that will forever please you. Amen!

Why it's important to be clean when we pray?

The only mirror that is going to show your true reflection is a clean one. Therefore, when you are clean you can be effective in your prayer life. Before one enters the Throne Room of God to present petitions, he himself must be clean. God said, in Job 22:30 TNKJV "He will even deliver one who is not innocent; yes, he will be delivered by the purity of your hands."

Testimony:

One day while praying for a prayer group I was in at that time, the Holy Spirit interrupted me. He let me know that when we came together to pray as a group that we were not in agreement. Well, at first I did not understand what He was talking about. (Because when praying with others at that time I stood on *Matthew 18:19* (NKJV) *"Again I say unto you, that if two of you shall agree on Earth as touching anything that they shall ask, it shall be done for them of My Father which is in Heaven."*

So, I asked The Holy Spirit, what did He mean? He said again, "you are not in agreement." Well, this time I quieted myself before The Lord to hear exactly what He meant.

I heard that "If I regard iniquity in my heart, The Lord will not hear me.

Psalm 66:18 (NKJV)

"Ye shall be holy for I the Lord Thy God am holy."

Leviticus 19:2 (KJV)

"Keep thy heart with all diligence for out of it flows the issues of life."

Proverbs 4:23(KJV)

After hearing God's Word spoken into my Spirit it became clear to me what He was telling me. At the time I was in an Intercessory Prayer Group made up of many different Christian Denominations. We came together once a month individually, collectively, and corporately as one before God. We prayed for the needs of our city, nation, and the World. But God said. "We were not in agreement."

The reason we were not in agreement according to God's standards is that we were all coming together as one man. In doing so, we needed to be received as one man by God. Before we could be in agreement and be heard as one before Him. We needed to repent and ask for forgiveness as one before Him.

The Lord showed me that there were some people in our midst actively engaged in sin. There was some there in the midst of sin. Some still had the residue of sin on them. These sins varied but all sin is unrighteousness in the sight of God. Therefore every last one of us needed to confess something prior to our coming before The Father as one to pray.

At that time The Prayer of Cleansing was instituted. When we confessed our sins as one man before God, then we were cleansed as one man before God. God therefore, received and heard us as one man coming before Him, thereby making us all in agreement in our prayers. I John 1:9 KJV

Whether you have been called into the ministry of Intercession or just doing your daily prayer time, asking God to forgive you, and you forgiving others, before you pray, can assure that you've been heard by God.

When a sink is clogged and the water won't go through the pipes, what do you do? Well, you try different means to resolve the problem. Dirty water sitting and not moving becomes stagnant. Therefore, it's important that there's a continual flow of the dirty water. Stagnant water creates a <u>foul</u> <u>odor!</u> <u>Therefore</u>, the clog must be removed from the pipes in order to get the water to flow properly. Our desire is to be a clean vessel that The Holy Spirit of God can flow through. We don't want to be a clogged up vessel or stench in God's Nostrils when we pray. Our vessels are the Temple of the Holy Spirit and to be used for the Glory of God. Don't remain clogged, with unconfessed sin, confess them.

In order to be effective in our prayer life we must be cleaned up often, for souls are at stake.

Don't allow pride to tell you that you're o.k. and have no sin. If we say that we have no sin, we are only fooling ourselves, and refusing to accept the Truth. I John 1:8 LB

Let's always humble ourselves before God, and ask Him to search our hearts, because He's the only one that knows what's in us anyway. God will, by His Holy Spirit show us what needs to be confessed. If you have been chosen specifically by God to be an Intercessor and a real prayer warrior for Him then there are certain guidelines we must follow.

Our responsibilities are:

1. *That our character be beyond reproach.*
2. *To walk in love no matter what.*
3. *To have and operate in the God kind of faith.*
4. *Always obey God.*

5. *Always forgive.*

6. *Put on the Whole Armor of God every-day.*

7. *Live a fasted lifestyle in every aspect of our lives.*

8. *To love and respect our neighbor as ourselves.*

9. *Be loyal to the ministry which God has placed you in respect and obey the leadership.*

10. *Be willing to lay down your life for the brethren.*

Prayer:

"Father in the Name of Jesus I come before you asking you to search my heart. I need you to plow up any and all fallow ground, to forgive me of any wrongs I've committed against you. Wash me with Your Word, cleanse me with The Blood of Jesus, and purge me with The Fire of The Holy Spirit. I forgive each and every person who

has harmed me in any way. I release them and ask You to bless them. Make me a vessel of honor to be used for Your Glory! Amen!

Thanksgiving and Praise in Prayer
(Please read this out loud)

"Let's enter into His gates with thanksgiving, and His courts with praise. Be thankful to Him, and bless His Name. For the Lord is good. His mercy is everlasting and His truth endures to all generations."

Psalm 100:4-5 KJV.

It is of utmost importance that we thank God every-day for His mercy and His grace. Where would we be without it?

What is being thankful? And what is thanksgiving? Webster defines it as this; An expression of gratitude; grateful acknowledgement of something received by or done for one. The act of giving thanks (formal often public) expression of thanks to God in the form of a prayer, etc.

Hallelujah! I want to express publicly before His people my heartfelt thanks to God, for His mighty miracles. All who are thankful should ponder them with me. His miracles demonstrate His honor, majesty, and eternal goodness.

Once we have prayed and made our requests known unto God, then thank Him for them. Do you know? That faith has been activated simply, by thanking God for the answer before the actual manifestation. That's why Jesus said in Mark 11:24 KJV, *"Therefore I say to you, whatever things you ask when you pray believe that you receive them, and you will have them."* Then it's only right to be thankful for them. Amen!

When we thank God in advance, that ensures our faith and total trust in Him. *"To do and to will of His own good pleasure concerning our request."* (I John 5:14-15

TN, KJV). *"Now this is the confidence that we have in Him. That if we ask anything according to His will, He hears us. And if we know that He hears us, whatever we ask, we know that we have the petitions that we have asked of Him."* We have something to be thankful for every-day, because, truly God is a good God.

When we praise God, we shame the devil. Praise used to be his job and he no longer has it, or can be received by God in the context of praise. Ezekiel 28:13-16 TNKJV says, *"You were in Eden, the Garden of God; every precious stone was your covering: The Sardius, Topaz, and Diamond, Beryl, Onyx, and Jasper, Sapphire, Turquoise, and Emerald with Gold. The workmanship of your timbrels and pipes was prepared for you on the day you were created. You were the anointed Cherub who covers; I established you; you* *were on The Holy Mountain of God; You walked back and forth in the midst of fiery stones. You were perfect in your ways from the day you were created, till <u>iniquity</u> was found in you. By the abundance of your trading you became filled with violence within, and you <u>sinned</u>; Therefore, I cast you as a profane thing out of The Mountain of God; And I <u>destroyed</u> you, o covering Cherub, from the midst of the fiery stones."*

So you see satan gets very angry with us when we praise God, for he can no longer do it, that's why he tries everything he can to stop our praise. But don't let him because its praise that gets you through the fire and the trials. When the tribulation come rejoice in the Lord always!!

Testimony:

There have been times when I started to pray and such heaviness would come upon me. I would be unable to open my mouth to pray or even allow The Holy Spirit to pray through me. After a long struggle of silence, my spirit started to sing a praise song to Jesus. `Jesus I love you, Jesus I praise you, Jesus I adore you and worship your name. Hallelujah! Well, suffice to say that heaviness left immediately. Afterward, there was such a sweet spirit surrounding me I was able to continue in my prayer time without interruption. When we concentrate on God everything else pales. Hallelujah!

"Sing a new song to The Lord! Sing it everywhere, around the World! Sing out His praises! Bless His name each day tell someone that He saves. Publish His glorious acts throughout the Earth. Tell everyone about the amazing things He does.

Psalm 96:1-3. LB

Hallelujah!   Hallelujah!   Hallelujah!
Hallelujah!   Hallelujah!   Hallelujah!

Hallelujah! Hallelujah! Bless the Lord for He is good!

Let's put the devil and all his cohorts on the run. Right now, we are going to bless the Lord! Amen!

Praise:

Dear God I exalt you. I glorify you. I magnify your Name. For You are the Omnipotent, Omnipresent, and Omniscient God. I bless Your Name Elohim, The Creator of the Heaven and the Earth, Who was in The Beginning. You are The Ancient of Days.

You are El Elyon, The Most High God. You are The Rose of Sharon, The Lily of The Valley, The Bright and Morning Star. You are all things to me, you are My God. You are The Everlasting Father. You are my Rock of Salvation. You're Yahweh

Shalom my Peace. Adonai, our Lord and Master. Yahweh Rapha, our healer. Yahweh Jirah our provider. We bless You, we blessYou , we bless You!

I love You Jesus, I love You Jesus, I love You Jesus, I love You Jesus, I love You Jesus, I love You Jesus, I love You Jesus, I love You Jesus, I love You Jesus, I love You Jesus!

Thank You Lord! How good You are! Your love and mercy continues on forever.

Glory! Glory! Glory! Glory! Glory! Glory! Glory! Glory! Glory! Glory! Glory! We praise You God for Your faithfulness, for Your goodness, for Your love, peace, life, health, strength, protection, favor.

Bless the Lord the God of Israel, who exist from everlasting ages past and on into everlasting eternity ahead. Amen and Amen bless His holy Name!

Worthy, oh worthy is the Lamb that was slain, bless His Name.

O Lord, our Lord, how excellent is Your Name in all the Earth. You who set Your glory above the Heavens. Jesus, Jesus, Jesus the name which is above every name, for every knee shall bow and every tongue shall confess to the glory of God the Name of the Lord Jesus Christ.

"Bless the Lord oh my soul; bless His holy Name! Bless the Lord, oh my soul and all that is within me, bless His holy Name! Bless the Lord oh my soul and forget not all His benefits."

Psalm 103:1-2 (LB.)
"Holy, Holy, Holy is the Lord. My soul says Holy, Holy, Holy."

Lord with all my heart I thank You. *"I will sing your praises before the armies of Angels in Heaven."*

Psalm 138:1 (LB.)

"Bless the Lord who is my immovable Rock. He gives me strength and skill in battle. He is always kind and loving to me; He is my Fortress my Tower of strength and safety, my Deliverer. He stands before me as a Shield. He subdues my people under me."

Psalm 144:1-2 LB

Hallelujah! Yes, praise the Lord! *"Praise Him in His Temple, and in the Heavens He made with mighty power. Praise Him for His mighty works. Praise His unequaled greatness. Praise Him with the Trumpet and with Lute and Harp. Praise Him with the Tambourines and Processional. Praise Him with stringed instruments and horns. Praise Him with the*

Cymbals, yes loud clanging Cymbals. Let everything alive give praises to the Lord! You praise Him! Hallelujah!"

Psalm 150 LB.

Prayer:

On bended knees I come, with a humble heart I come, bowing down at Your Holy Throne, as I lift my hands to you, and I pledge my life anew, I worship you in Spirit, I worship You in Truth, May my life be a praise unto You.

Obedience in Prayer

It's very important that we be obedient to God in all aspects of our lives. To be obedient is to know authority. Jesus is our example of obedience. All authority is given by God. If you do not recognize authority you then are not in obedience and therefore need to cry out for mercy. When we walk in obedience to God it is also a form of worship.

(Read I Kings Chapter 13)

This story is a good example of God's servant in obedience and disobedience. I believe God put this story in the Bible as a warning. To show us that we cannot have our own agendas or even listen to others regardless of who they are. If we have explicit instructions from God, what to do, how to do it, where to go and what to say then we must obey our instructions.

I call this Prophet the "no name" Prophet because I have not found any place in scripture where his name was given.

This no name Prophet of God knew exactly what he was supposed to do, but because someone who claimed to be from God told him something different to do. He allowed his flesh to obey man rather than God. *Acts 5:29b says: "We ought to obey God rather than men."* Always be watchful. For when God gives you explicit instructions the enemy will always send a distraction. Use the Wisdom of The Holy Spirit to know that if God spoke to you without that person before He is well capable of updating His instructions to you in a way that it will bear witness in your Spirit. Listen closely to the inner voice within you, which communicates with The

Spirit of God. If God has a proceeding word for previous instructions that He has already given, they will be revised in a way that there will be no question as to who is speaking. It's very possible that He will send someone to you but not before He tells you first.

Listen very carefully to The Holy Spirit of God and do what He says. Everyone with an Anointing, a title, or a position in the "Church" is not always exactly hearing from God. Sometimes people have their own agendas.

So as people of God we need to be in tune to God, especially, if what someone else says contradicts what God has already said and confirmed. Your very life could be on the line.

In Luke chapter 5, Jesus healed only one man, when all those other people were sick.

Why? The Jews confronted Jesus about healing the man on the Sabbath, because in their sight it was unlawful to do any work on that day. When they questioned Him about it, *Luke 5:19 (TNKJ) "Then answered Jesus and said unto them, verily, verily, I say unto you, the Son can do nothing of Himself, but what He seeth the Father do"*

For what things so ever He doeth, these also doeth the Son likewise. In other words Jesus basically told them He did not care what they thought or said. He did what His Father did. Now, in some situations and circumstances that's the attitude we have to take, when we know specifically what The Father has told us to do.

Caution:

When we take this attitude, let's make sure that you don't have your own agenda and cross over into disobedience

Prayer:

"Oh mighty God have mercy upon me, forgive me for the times I have been disobedient in anything you gave me to do. Help me Father in Jesus' name by Your Holy Spirit get in a place of total obedience unto You. No matter what I want to please You. Amen!"

Why we must pray?

We must pray because Jesus prayed, and is still praying.

Prayer is our line of communication to God. It's where we talk to God and He talks back to us. It's a dialogue when we talk to Him He answers, His answers to us are instructions in life. He's not giving us an option to obey His instructions or not but He's telling us the solution to the problem that was brought to Him by us. Since He is the only one that knows our hearts and everything about us from the beginning to the end, we should obey His instructions. Why go to God in prayer and not do what He tells you to do?

We must be obedient to God, operating in the love of God, having the discipline of God, knowing the will of God and exercising God kind of faith. To do all these things takes the character of Jesus. You get the character of Jesus by spending time with Him in prayer.

It takes sacrifice and dedication to pray and have compassion for others and not always think about ourselves. Jesus' concern was always for the other person, He always put Himself last. Every Intercessor (true) knows that as they pray for others that God concerns Himself with their own personal needs.

Testimony:

Not long ago we had no income and was totally trusting and believing God to meet our needs daily. On this particular day I was tired, not so much physically but just tired. Those of you who have been in the fire know what I'm talking about, one of those days where you are just tired. Well, in the midst of the tired the Holy Spirit spoke to my heart and said, "fall on your face and pray in the Spirit for someone else's need", I did what He told me. It's a blessing just to hear God speak to you and to be used by Him. As I continued to pray and project love for this other person, the phone rang, and as a rule when I'm praying the phone is always turned off. I do not allow any distractions during prayer time. Well, this time the phone was different I did not get a chance to turn off the phone prior to praying. My husband did not answer the phone for whatever reason, so it just kept ringing. Finally, I asked God, should I answer? He said, "Yes". When I answered it was someone offering me a job that I had not even applied for. Praise God!!

One of the most famous prayers Jesus prayed while here on Earth is recorded in (John 17:21-22 L.B.) My prayer for all of them is that they will be of one heart and mind, just as You and I are, Father that just as you are in me and I am in You, so they will be in Us, and the World will believe You sent Me. I have given them the glory you gave me, the glorious unity of being one as we are. I in them and You in Me, all being perfected into one so that the World will know You sent Me and will understand that You love them as much as you love me.

Jesus wants His Church to be one, bonded together in love and unity. We must pray till we all come in the unity of the faith, and of the knowledge of the Son of God, unto a perfect man, unto the measure of the stature of the fullness of Christ: (Ephesians 4:13, KJV)

God has called His church to unity. If the church as a whole would just slow down and hear what Jesus meant, we wouldn't have any problem just coming together just to pray.

When I first became a Christian I was truly born again and believed that the church was <u>one.</u> It was a shocking revelation to find out that it wasn't. This needs to be changed so when those future believers Jesus prayed for in John 17, come into the Kingdom, they'll know what the true meaning of <u>love</u> and <u>unity</u> is.

To those Intercessors, that are praying for the unity of The Body of Christ be encouraged, to stand steadfast, believing that there is one Body, and one Spirit, even as you are called in one hope of your calling; one Lord, one Faith, and one baptism, one God and Father of all, Who is above all, and through all, and in you all. (Ephesians 4:4-6 King James)

Prayer:

Father, forgive us for any part we played in keeping Your Body divided, let your light shine on the dark areas of division in our midst, give us revelation knowledge of how to come together as one in love and unity. Plow up the fallow ground in each of our hearts in every area that has caused us to be divided. Give us the mercy and the grace it's going to take to walk in Your True Love. Bless us to show the World that we are the <u>One</u> that will show forth Your glory in this Earth. In Jesus' Name, Amen!

When should we pray?

Pray all the time. Ask God for anything in line with the Holy Spirit's wishes. Plead with Him reminding Him of your needs, and keep praying ernestly for all Christians everywhere. (Ephesians 6:18 L.B)

I have set watchmen on your walls, O Jerusalem, who shall never hold their peace day or night. You who make mention of the Lord do not keep silent, [and everyone that's been born again has that right not to give God any rest. With the condition that our World is in today us Christians need to be before the Father and] give no rest till He establishes and till He makes Jerusalem a praise in the Earth. (Isaiah 62:6-7 King James)

As Christians our life line is prayer. There are many times, types, methods, places, and positions to pray, but we need to always pray no matter what. As we pray Jesus intercepts our prayers.

Our prayers are handled very carefully when they reach Heaven in *(Revelation 8:3-6 KJV)* *"Then another Angel came and stood at the Alter, having a golden censer; and there was given unto Him much incense, that he should offer it with the prayers of all the Saints upon the Golden Alter which was before the Throne. And the smoke of the incense, which came with the prayers of the Saints, ascended up before God out of the angel's hand.*

Then the angel took the censer, filled it with fire from the Alter, and threw it to the Earth. And there were noises, thundering's, lightning's, and an earthquake."

To everything there is a season, and a time to every purpose under the Heaven. (Ecclesiastes 3:1) It surely is time to pray for our loved ones, leaders of the Church, the unity of families, Government leaders, educational institutions, professors police, military (all branches), prison officials, prisoners, the youth our neighborhoods, our city, nation and the world.

The types of prayers we are to pray are prayers with the distinctive characteristic of Jesus. In (Matthew 6:9-13 K.J.V.) is the model prayer. *"After this manner therefore pray ye: Our Father which art in Heaven, hallowed be thy name. Thy Kingdom come. Thy will be done in Earth, as it is in Heaven. Give us this day our daily bread. And forgive us our debts as we forgive our debtors. And lead us not into temptation but deliver us from evil: For thine is the*

Kingdom, and the power, and the glory, forever, Amen".

Another type of prayer is found in *(James 5:15-16 KJV) "And the prayer of faith shall save the sick and the Lord shall raise Him up; and if he have committed sins, they shall be forgiven him. Confess your faults one to another, and pray one for another, that ye may be healed. The effectual fervent prayer of a righteous man availeth much."*

The prayer of thanksgiving, prayer of praise, prayer of cleansing, prayer of exhortation, intercessory prayer and prayers of supplication are different types of prayers. But when you pray trust the Holy Spirit to lead and guide you how to pray. Romans 8:26-27 K.J.V says, *"Likewise, the Spirit also helpeth our infirmities: For we know not what we should pray for as we ought but the Spirit Himself maketh intercession for us with groanings which cannot be uttered, and he that searcheth the hearts knoweth what is the mind of the Spirit, because He maketh intercession for the saints according to the will of God."*

God is a God of order and the most important method we should use is to be disciplined in our personal relationship and identifing with the role we have with Him. We are co-laborers with Jesus. Always remember that the Holy Spirit is in total control and when we move as he moves our method will always be right.

There are many places to pray in Matthew 6:6, KJV *"But thou when thou prayest, enter into thy closet, and when thou hast shut thy door, pray to thy Father which is in secret; And thy Father which seeth in secret shall reward thee openly."*

The best place for me to pray is in my secret closet, I feel so free and open to speak and the Father speaks back to me.

"I will therefore that men pray everywhere, lifting up holy hands, without wrath and doubting."

I Timothy 2:8 KJV

Here are some ideas of places we can pray:

In bed, in the bathroom, while doing housework, cooking, in the car, on our jobs, during breaks, walking in the neighborhood, at family gatherings just steal away to yourself and pray, while shopping, on elevators, your place of worship, there are many more places to pray, the key is to just pray in whatever place the Holy Spirit leads you. God is more personally concerned with the condition of our hearts when we pray rather so much the place.

"And when ye stand praying, forgive, if ye have an ought against any that your Father also which is in Heaven may forgive you your trespasses. But if you do not forgive, neither will your Father which is in Heaven forgive your trespasses."

Mark 11:25-26 KJV

Prayer:

Dear Heavenly Father, help me to always forgive anyone who harms me in any way so that I can be forgiven by You. And forgive me for not praying when there were opportunities to and I didn't. From this moment forward I ask you Father in Jesus' name to help me to be more sensitive in the area of prayer. I make myself available to pray anywhere, anyplace, and at any-time according to your will Father and not mine. Amen!

Our Position in Prayer

One of the positions we are to take in prayer is that of a soldier armed and ready for battle.

"Therefore take up the Whole Armor of God, so that you may be able to withstand in the evil day, and having done all to stand. Stand therefore, having girded your waist with Truth, having put on the Breastplate of Righteousness, and having Shod your feet with the preparation of the gospel of Peace; above all taking the Shield of Faith with which you will be able to quench all the fiery darts of the wicked one. And take the Helmet of Salvation, and the Sword of the Spirit, which is the Word of God." Praying always with all prayer and supplication in the Spirit, being watchful to this end with all perseverance and supplication for all the saints-and for me, that utterance may be

given to me, that I may open my mouth boldly to make known the mystery of the gospel, for which I am an ambassador in chains; that in it I may speak boldly, as I ought to speak.

Ephesians 6:10-20 NKJV & NSFLB

The word "put" in this scripture is a Verb and a Verb is an action word, something we have to do thereby corresponding with James 1:22 TN, KJV. *"But be doers of the Word and not just hears only, deceiving yourselves."*

Every day we are to literally put on the Whole Armor of God, by taking this act of faith in the natural realm it activates the supernatural realm. We are then putting works to our faith. (James 2:17) (TN, KJV) Thus also, faith by itself, (if it does not have works) is dead.

The reason we have to put the Whole Armor of God on every day is because the natural body gets tired and weary therefore, must take time out for rest. In the process of resting, we have a tendency to get real comfortable in our flesh. In the midst of being comfortable one might loosen (*The Truth*) their Girdle, let down their (*Faith*) Shield, and lay down their (*Word*) Sword etc. You see the point that I'm making is that it's of the strictest importance that we put the "Whole Armor of God" on every day.

God has given us these special weapons because a war and a battle is waged against the Saints of God in the Spirit Realm therefore, we are not to take them lightly. *"For we do not wrestle against flesh and blood, but against principalities, against powers, against the rulers of the darkness of this age, against spiritual host of wickedness in the heavenly places."*

Ephesians 6:12 (TN, KJV)

"Finally, my brethren, be strong in the Lord and the power of His might."

Ephesians 6:10 (TN, KJV)

Throughout the Gospels when Jesus encountered the devil or demons He did not go through a lot of changes. He simply spoke the Word to the devil and cast out the demons. Be like Jesus!

When we do spiritual warfare we must have violent faith, because we're taking back that which the enemy has stolen. Do you think he's (the devil) going to give it up easily no, no, no, he's not!!

"And from the days of John the Baptist until now the Kingdom of Heaven suffers violence, and the violent take it by force."

Matthew 11:12, TN, KJ

Now this scripture has a two-fold meaning, we use it when we attack the powers of darkness that invade our supernatural space, and we have used it to get from the Kingdom that which men wanted to use and then operate the principles from their intellect. There is no way men should be using God's Spiritual principles and try to incorporate them with their intellect. *Man's intellect and The "KINGDOM OF GOD" are two totally different Realms.*

It's time that we as children of the Most High God Who has all Power in His Hand, start to exercise the Authority that Jesus invested in us!

"Behold, I give you the Authority to trample on serpents and scorpions, and over all the power of the enemy and nothing shall by any means hurt you."

Luke 10:19 TN, KJV

"Ask of Me, and I shall give thee the heathen for thine inheritance, and the uttermost parts of the Earth for thy possession."

Psalm2:8 (KJV)

Go in and possess your land, start within your own home. Turn the television off, hang up the phone, put down those calorie, laden snacks, and walk in "True Love", not superficial love. One sure way of getting the victory over the devil is to always walk in True Love. When some demons saw Jesus coming they started crying out before He even said anything to them. That's because Jesus is the essence of

Love and that Love petrifies the devil and his demons every time.

We must speak the Word of God:

"For the Word of God is living and powerful, and sharper than any two-edged sword, piercing even to the division of soul and spirit, and of joints and morrow, and is a discerner of the thoughts and intents of the heart."

(Hebrews 3:12) (TN, KJV)

Testimony:

One morning in the wee hours between 3:00 & 4:00 a.m., the Holy Spirit awakened me. He told me to look on the sides of my bed. When I looked there were demons that had the heads of Humans and the bodies of snakes. At first I was startled, but that passed quickly. For I know who I am in Jesus Christ and that I'm covered by "His Blood!"

My instructions from the Holy Spirit were to get up out of bed and step over all this evil, go into the bathroom and stand inside of the bathtub. After I stood in the bathtub the Holy Spirit showed me why they had come. Their mission was to try and hinder me from accomplishing that which God had given me to do. God let me know if I followed His instructions that these particular wicked spirits would never be able to bother me again. Well once I was inside the bathtub (by the way it's still dark for no lights had been turned on) a dome of light came down over me, it sealed me inside. Then God said, "Now take the Sword (His Word) and reach out". When I reached outside of the lighted dome with the Sword which is symbolic of His Word the Sword became light. As I would reach outside of the dome with the Sword striking the enemy, the Sword of light would cut away all the darkness. This went on for quite some time, I could hear screams in the spirit as the Sword cut them and they fell. To God be the glory!!

Note: To those of you who may be thinking at this moment "I don't believe that." Don't be so quick to judge for you do not know what you're going to encounter when you make a decision to stand for God and go as high as he allows you to go in the Spirit Realm. **It's real!** *"And they overcame him by the BLOOD of the LAMB and by the word of their testimony, and they did not love their lives to the death."*

Revelation 12:11 (TN, KJV)

✷ Speak God's Word no matter what! *I Timothy 4:1-5 says, "I charge you therefore before God and the Lord Jesus Christ who will judge the living and the dead, at His appearing and His Kingdom: Preach the Word! Be ready in season and out of season. Convince, rebuke, exhort, with all longsuffering and teaching. For the time will come when they will not endure sound doctrine but according to their own desires, because they have itching ears, they will heap up for themselves teachers; and they will turn their ears away from the Truth and be turned aside to fables. But you be watchful in all things, endure afflictions, do the work of an Evangelist, fulfill your ministry."*

What does "speak" mean?

Speak - To make or give out sound, to utter words orally to speak freely or forcefully. This is the definition to use when speaking the Word of God. When we speak God's Word say it out loud so every demon and satan himself can hear.

God has given us authority to condemn every word that has been spoken against us. *"No weapon formed against you shall prosper, and every tongue which rises against you in judgement you shall condemn. This is the heritage of the servants of the LORD, and their righteousness is from me, says the LORD. "*

Isaiah 54:17, (TN, KJV)

Many of us have gone around in circles unable to accomplish anything because of the words that people have spoken over us. They were not words that God says about us. Therefore, our lives were affected in many different ways that were negative. Now is the time to come against all those negative words said about us. Say this prayer out aloud:

Prayer:

In the Name of Jesus, I snatch every word out of the atmosphere that has been spoken over me in a negative connotation! I curse their very existence at the root, and command them to die for they are rendered powerless and ineffective! I curse them from the past, the present, and the future, the spoken word, the written word, the action, the thought or the deed! Because the BLOOD of JESUS prevails against them!!!! Amen!

Now you are free to be established in the things of God, to do that which He has ordained for you to do.

Let's activate God's Word and His Promises in our lives now, for He said, *"This word that I speak shall surely come to pass. So also is My Word. I send it out and it always produces fruit. It shall accomplish all I want it to, and prosper everywhere I send it. You will live in joy and peace. The mountains and hills the trees of the field, all the world around you will rejoice!*

Isaiah 55:11-12 (LB)

This is God's Word to Zerubbabel, *"not by might nor by power, but by my Spirit, says the Lord of hosts you will succeed because of my Spirit, though you are few and weak."*

Zechariah 4:6 (KJV)

"And I tell you this, whatever you bind on Earth is bound in Heaven, and whatever you

free on Earth is free in Heaven. "I also tell
you this if two of you agree down here on
Earth concerning anything down here on
Earth concerning anything you ask for, my
Father in Heaven will do it for you".

Matthew 18:18-19 (LB)

"He who dwells in the secret place of the
Most High shall abide under the shadow of
the Almighty. I will say of the Lord, He is my
refuge and my fortress; My God in Him I
will trust".

Psalms 91:1-2 TN, KJV

And He said unto them, "go into all, the
World and preach the Gospel to every
creature. He who believes and is baptized
will be saved, but he who does not believe
will be condemned. And these signs will
follow those who believe: In My name they
will cast out demons; They will speak with
new tongues; They will take up serpents;

and if they drink anything deadly, it will by no means hurt them; they will lay hands on the sick, and they will recover."

Mark 16:15-18 (TN, KJV)

Moreover, it is required in stewards that one be found faithful.

I Corinthians 4:2 KJV

"But you shall receive power when the Holy Spirit has come upon you; and you shall be witnesses to me in Jerusalem, and in Judea and Samaria and to the end of the Earth."

Acts 1:8 (KJV)

"The Lord is my light and my salvation; whom shall I fear? The Lord is the strength of my life; of whom shall I be afraid? When the wicked come against me to eat up my flesh, my enemies and foes, they stumbled and fell, though an army should encamp against me, my heart shall not fear. Though

war should rise against me, in this I will be confident."

Psalm 27:1-3 (KJV)

I cried out to God with my voice to God with my voice; and He gave ear to me. In the day of my trouble I sought the Lord;

Psalm 77:1-2a. (TN, KJV)

The righteous cry out, and the Lord hears, and delivers them out of all their troubles.

Psalm 34:17 (TN, KJV)

I shall not die, but live to declare the works of the Lord. The lord has chastened me severely, but He has not given me over to death.

Psalm 118:17 (TN, KJV)

Greater is He that is in me* than he that is in the World.

1 John 4:4 (KJV)

*Note: The word (me) in this scripture is in the singular and it's also a personal pronoun denoting one person; whereas, the word (world) is in the plural which includes all worldly powers. Just think, that very same Power that is within you is greater than all the power in the World. Praise God, it is mind boggling!

When you make a decision as to whose side you are on, get ready for everything around you to explode. You will be lied on, persecuted, ostracized, and suffer in areas you've never dreamed of before. You will be put into the fire and I mean fire! This power I'm talking about does not come just because you go to church and you are a "good" Christian. This power only comes when you have been through the fire and not around it. The fire comes to burn out all those things in us that are not of God. Once you've been purged and passed your test of fire then and only then does God uses you. When the cares of this World does not matter any- more you are now a terror to the devil and his cohorts.

Suffering is a part of having Power with God. Think about Jesus.

"Therefore, since Christ suffered for us in the flesh, arm yourselves also with the same mind, for he who has suffered in the flesh has ceased from sin. That he no longer should live the rest of his time in the flesh for the lusts of men, but for the will of God."

I Peter 4:1-2 (TN, KJV)

When you suffer for God He gets the glory.

"Beloved, do not think it strange concerning the fiery trial which is to try you, as though some strange thing happened to you; but, rejoice to the extent that you partake of Christ's sufferings, that when His glory is

revealed, you may also be glad with exceeding joy."

I Peter 4:12-13 (TN, KJV)

Since we know who we are as Christians, and because of what Jesus have done for us, we can now go to the drawing board and plan our strategies.

Prayer:

Dear Heavenly Father, I humble myself and come to you in the name of Jesus, asking You to make me a soldier in Your Army because I am now willing to participate in the fight. Help me to prepare myself for whatever front you decide to put me on. Give me the ability to stand with my Whole Armor on. Even in the face of any and all adversities knowing that You will never leave me nor forsake me. And to always walk in love. Amen!

Prayers of distinction to be prayed every-day or as needed:

1. Cleansing Prayers
2. Prayer to Renew your mind
3. Prayer for prosperity
4. Prayer of forgiveness
5. Prayer for healings, physical, spiritual, emotional, mental, financial
6. Prayer against the wiles of the devil
7. Prayer for the backslider

Cleansing Prayers:

Father according to Your Word, pride goes before destruction and a haughty spirit before a fall. It is better to be of a humble spirit with the meek and poor, then to divide the spoil with the proud. Father in the name of Jesus help me to resist pride and haughtiness which comes before disaster, and put on humility which precedes honor. Just as Jesus humbled Himself as a Servant and carried his obedience to death even the death of the Cross. Help me Father to be Your humble servant and not allow pride and arrogance to be a part of me. As I humble myself under Your Mighty Hand, give me Your grace that You may exalt me in Your own time. Thank You, for the reward of humility and the reverent and worshipful fear of the LORD which is riches, honor, and life. For Lord You have created in me a clean heart and renewed a right preserving and steadfast spirit within me Therefore, I cleanse my ways by taking heed and keeping watch on myself according to Your Word, conforming my life to it. Since, Your great promises are mine I cleanse myself from everything that contaminates and defiles my spirit, soul, and body, and bring my consecration to completeness in the reverential fear of God. With my whole heart have I sought You LORD, Oh let me not wander or step aside either in ignorance or willfully from Your Commandments. Your Word have I laid up in my heart that I might not sin against You. Thank You Jesus for cleansing me with Your Blood. Amen!

Oh wise and Omnipotent, Omniscience, and Omnipresent God. I come before You because of Your Auspicious Grace, thanking You for Your mercy, and grace, Your love, peace, health, joy, hope a sound mind the anointing and salvation. For You are the Alpha and the Omega the beginning and You are the ending. The everlasting Father, the mighty Prince of Peace, the Rose of Sharon and the Lily of the valley, the Bright and morning Star. You're El Elyon the Most High God, because You alone are God!! I bless You, I magnify You I glorify and praise Your Holy name for You alone are worthy!!

I can do nothing without You so I come now in the name of Your precious Son Jesus asking You to manifest Your Presence in my midst today. For where the Presence of the Lord is there is liberty, and I need liberality in You Oh God!!! I ask You to shine Your Light on every hidden area of my heart, to expose everything that's not like You. To plow up fallow ground root up hatred, bitterness, un-forgiveness, malice, strife, arrogance and pride. Send Your Word to wash me cleanse me with the Blood of Jesus, purge me with the Fire of the Holy Spirit that I may be a vessel of honor to be used for Your glory!! As I stand at the crossroads and look asking where the good way is and walking in it, thank You that I will find rest and peace in my soul. Thank You Father for forgiving me and I receive my forgiveness by faith in Jesus' name. Amen!!

Forgive me Father for the sin of omission and the sin of commission, as I forgive everyone who has trespassed against me. I know that if I do not forgive You will not forgive me. Have mercy on me O LORD for not loving my neighbor as I love myself. Wash me with Your Word and cleanse me with the Blood of Jesus. Purge me with a coal from Your very Altar and Throne Room. Since I am a person of unclean lips and dwell in the midst of a people of *unclean lips; allow Your Holy Seraphim to lay that coal on my mouth so when it touches my lips; my iniquity will be taken away and the Fire of the Holy Spirit in me will cause all of my sins to be purged. I have confessed my sins, according to Your Word in I John 1:9. If I confess my sins You are faithful and just to forgive me my sins and cleanse me from all unrighteousness. Keep me in reverential fear of You Oh LORD! I receive my forgiveness by faith and thank You for it in Jesus' name Amen!!*

Prayer to renew your mind:
Father I dedicate my mind to You. I ask, in Jesus' name to be transformed today by the renewing of my mind. I ask You to take away everything that's not of You, wash my mind make it clean purify it, soak it out, flush it off that I may prove what is that good and acceptable and perfect will of

God. For I want to be used by You. I want Your Holy Spirit to rule and reign through me as You so please in Jesus' name Amen!!

Prayer for Prosperity:

Father in the name of Jesus, I pray according to Your Word in Matthew 6:10, Thy Kingdom come Thy will be done on earth as it is in heaven. You said, "Whatsoever I declare it shall be established unto me. So I declare in the name of Jesus that I am a Child of God and a Heir of God and a Joint-Heir with Jesus, He owns everything for it all belongs to Him therefore, it belongs to me also. Health, wholeness, peace and riches are mine because Your blessings are upon me. Since You delight in the prosperity of Your servants I declare that I am prosperous in every area of my life. So I command my wealth to come from the North South East and West. Manifest yourself now. All money and any tangible items that I may need to make my life whole in every aspect. Manifest now for my money has a mission. To pay Tithes and give offerings give into the lives of those who have a need without question compromise, or judging. To give into ministries that's promoting the Kingdom of God and getting souls saved. To give to Israel to help bring back the Jews from all around the world back to Jerusalem. In Yeshua's name, Amen!

Forgiveness Prayer:

And forgive us our debts, as we forgive our debtors.

Father, I forgive everyone who has trespassed against me so that You can forgive me my trespasses. If I forgive the sins of anyone they are forgiven; if I retain the sins of anyone they are retained.

Father Your Word says to Love your enemies and pray for those who persecute you. I come before You in Jesus' name to lift up_____
before You. I invoke blessings upon them and pray for their happiness.

Father not only will I pray for_____, but I set myself to treat them well, be merciful, sympathetic, tender responsive and compassionate toward_____ even as You are father. I thank You that I can do all things through Christ who strengthens me.

Father I thank You that as I forgive_____ that You would render their hearts and not their garments, that they will be aware of the error of their ways and be convicted by Your Holy Spirit. And turn from their wicked ways, have a repentant heart and come to the knowledge of Your Word also.

And now Father I roll this work upon You commit and trust it wholly to You; and believe that you will cause my thoughts to become in agreement to Your will, and my plans shall be established and succeed in Jesus' name Amen!

Prayer against the wiles of the devil:

I believe God! And it is counted unto me for righteousness (Romans 4:3).

"For You O LORD will bless the righteous; with favor You will surround him as with a shield."

Psalm 5:12

"Heaven and earth will pass away every jot and tittle but My Words by no means shall pass away."

Matthew 24:35

Now I come Father, in the name of Jesus speaking Your Word over every negative situation and every negative circumstance.

"Behold, I give unto you power to tread on serpents and scorpions and over all the power of the enemy: and nothing shall by any means hurt you."

Luke 10:19

We have the authority yet we still have to contend with the enemy.

"For we wrestle not against flesh and blood, but against principalities, against powers, against the rulers of the darkness of this world, against spiritual wickedness in high places."

Ephesians 6:12

Therefore, I am not afraid of what the enemy can do to me;

"For God has not given me the spirit of fear; but of power, and of love, and of a sound mind."

2 Timothy 1:7

I am victorious because I have the greatest helper with me at all times:

"Behold God is my helper:"

(Psalm 54:4)

"Behold, the LORD God will help me; who is he that shall condemn me?"

(Isaiah 50:9)

"What then shall we say to these things? If God is for us, who can be against us?"

(Romans 8:31)

I am prosperous in every area of my life:
"The blessing of the LORD, makes rich, and He adds no sorrows with it. (Proverbs 10:22) for it is God that gives me power to get wealth, that He may establish His Covenant which He swore unto our fathers.

(Deuteronomy 8:18)

God is my refuge, He is my protector:
"No weapon formed against me shall prosper and every tongue spoken against me in judgement I shall condemn, for I am

the servant of the Most High God and my
righteousness is of Him says the LORD!"

Isaiah 54:17

I am a holy vessel:
"Be ye holy for I the LORD thy God is
holy.

Leviticus 19:2

"Pursue peace with all people, and without
holiness no man shall see the LORD."

Hebrews 12:1

"I know that all things work together for
good to those who love God, to those who
are called according to His purpose."

Romans 8:28

"Because I have set my love upon God,
therefore God will deliver me; God will set
me on high, because I have known His
name (Jesus). I shall call upon Jesus and

Jesus will answer me. Jesus will be with me in trouble; Jesus will deliver me and honor me. With long life Jesus will satisfy me and show me His Salvation.

(Psalm 91:14-16)
Amen!

(Given by the Holy Spirit to Evangelist Vera Armstrong January 10, 2006)

Prayer for the Backslider:

Father in the name of Jesus I humble myself under Your mighty hands. I ask You to wash me with Your Word, cleanse me with the Blood of Jesus. Lord, purge me with the Fire of the Holy Spirit and make me a vessel of honor to be used for Your glory! Father, You said, I shall declare a thing and it shall be established unto me so my light will shine on my ways. Not only let my light shine LORD, but let my salt season, so that one who is guilty will be delivered by the purity of my hands. Father, I come into Your presence to seek and to save those that are lost. I thank You for the heathen as my inheritance and the uttermost parts of the earth for my possession. I yield myself as an instrument of love because it is love and kindness that will draw them to you. Give me Your divine wisdom and divine knowledge to minister to each person individually. I pray they be reconnected to You by Your Holy Spirit. As they come, Father I thank You that they will render their hearts and not their garments. The spirit of conviction and repentance will cause them to say yes to Your will and yes to Your way. Help them to be renewed in the spirit of their minds to seek Your Face; in order to be doers of Your Word and not just hearers only. Shower down Your mercy and grace O LORD. Let the purpose for which each one is called be fulfilled. Give them the ability to be steadfast in You. Cause them to shake off everything that's not like You. When they are weak give them grace to say they are strong. It is You God that girds us with strength and makes our way perfect. Father You sent Your Word and healed them and delivered them from all their destructions. Father, heal them physically, spiritually emotionally, mentally, financially, socially, intellectually

*and economically for Your glory in Jesus'
name.*

Amen!!!

We must **exercise** declarations that are based on the Word of God. These declarations are who and what we are, in Jesus Christ. The foundation Scriptures are, *John 1:1-5, 14.*

Exercise!

In the Word I have life! (Psalm 119:25; I John 5:12)

In the Word I have Eternal Life! (I John 5:11, 18)

In the Word I have Justification! (Romans 5:16)

In the Word I have Peace! (Isaiah 26:3)

In the Word I have Love! (Romans 5:5)

In the Word I have Grace! (Luke 2:40; 2 Corinthians 13:14)

In the Word I have no Condemnation! (Romans 8:1)

In the Word I am Free! (Romans 8:2)

In the Word I am a Child of God! (John 1:12)

In the Word I am an Heir of God! (Romans 8:17)

In the Word I am a Joint-Heir with Christ! (Romans 8:17)

In the Word I am more than a Conqueror! (Romans 8:37)

In the Word I am satisfied! (Isaiah 53:11; Jeremiah 31:14)

In the Word I am enriched in all Knowledge! (I Corinthians 1:5)

In the Word I have wisdom! (James 1:5)

In the Word I have Righteousness! (Isaiah 45:24; 2Corinthians 5:21)

In the Word I have Redemption! (Ephesians 1:7)

In the Word I have "VICTORY OVER DEATH!" I Corinthians 15:54)

In the Word I am Established! (Colossians 2:7; Hebrews 13:9)

In the Word I am Anointed! (2 Corinthians1:21)

In the Word I <u>always</u> Triumph! (2 Corinthians 2:14)

In the Word I have a Renewed Mind! (Ephesians 4:23)

In the Word I am a New Creation! (2 Corinthians 5:17)

In the Word I am an Ambassador of God! (2 Corinthians 5:20)

In the Word I have Liberty! (Galatians 5:1)

In the Word I am Redeemed from the curse of the Law! (Galatians 3:13)

In the Word I have the blessings of Abraham! (Galatians 3:14)

In the Word I overcome the devil, the flesh and the world! (I John 6:5; Revelation 12:11)

In the Word I am a Son of God! (Galatians 4:7)

In the Word I have the God kind of Faith! (Romans 10:17)

In the Word I was created for Good Works! (2 Timothy 2:21)

In the Word I have Boldness! (I John 4:17)

In the Word I do not worry! (Matthew 6:25; 34)

In the Word I can be obedient! (I Peter 1:14)

In the Word I have Strength! (Psalm 27:1; Jeremiah 16:19a)

In the Word I am Sanctified! (John 17:19; I Corinthians 1:2)

In the Word I am delivered! (Romans 7:6)
In the Word I have Forgiveness! (Acts 26:18)
In the Word I can Forgive Others! (Matthew 6:12)

In the Word I have Mercy! (Luke 1:50; Romans 11:32)

In the Word I am Complete and Perfect! (2 Corinthians 13:9; John 17:23; Colossians 1:28)

In the Word I have Joy unspeakable! (John 17:13)

In the Word I am Settled! (Psalm 119:89)

Be perfect, as God is perfect! (Matt 5:48)

In the Word I have no fear! (2 Timothy 1:7; I John 4:18)

In the Word I am Healed Physically, Spiritually, Emotionally, Financially, Mentally Socially, Intelligently and Economically! (Isaiah 53:4-5)

In the Word I am Strong in the Power of God's Might! (Ephesians 6:10)

In the Word I have the High Calling of God! (I Thessalonians 4:7)

In the Word I am a Holy priest of God! (I Peter 2:5)

In the Word I am made Whole! (Colossians 2:9-10)

In the Word I can do All Things! (Philippians 4:13)

In the Word I am the Favor of God! (Psalm 5:12; Proverbs 12:2)

In the Word I have Divine Protection! (Psalm 91)

In the Word I have Understanding! (Psalm 119:130)

In the Word I have Victory! (I Corinthians 15:57)

In the Word I know God! (2 Timothy 1:12, 2:25; I John 3:24)

About the Author

Vera Armstrong describes herself as a person who has always just loved people, and when God called her to do a work for Him she responded with here I am Lord send me. Galatians 2:20 is her Rhema Word that catapulted her to go.

During the 29 years of her salvation she has encouraged 100s of people to pray. She has led many prayer walks through her city and reclaimed territory for Jesus. She has laid Foundational Truths in many a Christian who has now gone on with God fulfilling their potential. She graduated 7 classes of students from The Abundant Life Understanding God and His Covenants Class. She was the Administrative Secretary with The United Prayer Intercessors for 10 years and worked diligently until God promoted her. She served what she calls her "Boot Camp" years at the Straight Gate

International Church with her beloved Bishop Andrew and Pastor Viveca Merritt.

This book was written in Vera's 9th year of Salvation but is just now going to print. She says, "all the suffering had not been complete for this work to be published but now the price has been paid."

Hallelujah!!